NORTHGATE LIBRARY

JUL -- 2016

NO LONGER PROPERTY OF
SEATTLE PUBLIC LIBRA

D0602960

Summer

Julie Murray

Abdo
SEASONS
Kids

abdopublishing.com

Published by Abdo Kids, a division of ABDO, PO Box 398166, Minneapolis, Minnesota 55439.
Copyright © 2016 by Abdo Consulting Group, Inc. International copyrights reserved in all countries.
No part of this book may be reproduced in any form without written permission from the publisher.

Printed in the United States of America, North Mankato, Minnesota.

052015

092015

THIS BOOK CONTAINS
RECYCLED MATERIALS

Photo Credits: iStock, Shutterstock

Production Contributors: Teddy Borth, Jennie Forsberg, Grace Hansen

Design Contributors: Candice Keimig, Dorothy Toth

Library of Congress Control Number: 2014958403

Cataloging-in-Publication Data

Murray, Julie.
 Summer / Julie Murray.
  p. cm. -- (Seasons)
ISBN 978-1-62970-921-5
Includes index.
1. Summer--Juvenile literature. 2. Seasons--Juvenile literature.   I. Title.
508.2--dc23
                    2014958403

Table of Contents

Summer

Summer is one of the

four seasons.

Spring

Summer

Winter

Fall

5

The air is hot in summer.

The days are long.

The leaves are green.

The flowers are colorful.

Gardens grow in summer.

Finn **picks** the tomatoes.

Animals try to stay cool.

The cow rests in the **shade**.

Summer can be fun!

Julia likes to fish.

Lucy plays at the beach.

John swims in the pool.

Addy **enjoys** a picnic.

Ryan plays baseball.

What will you do this summer?

Summer Fun

blow bubbles

go to the playground

go on a bike ride

go to the pool

Glossary

enjoy
to have a good time.

shade
an area where there is little light because something is blocking the sun.

pick
to gather by plucking.

Index

abdokids.com

Use this code to log on to abdokids.com and access crafts, games, videos, and more!

Abdo Kids Code:
SSK9215